THE BEST OF POUCHER'S SCOTLAND

BOOKS BY W. A. POUCHER

Overleaf: Sgurr Nan Gobhar

THE BEST OF
POUCHER'S SCOTLAND

W. A. POUCHER

CONSTABLE · LONDON

FIRST PUBLISHED IN GREAT BRITAIN 1996 BY CONSTABLE & COMPANY LIMITED
3 THE LANCHESTERS, 162 FULHAM PALACE ROAD, LONDON W6 9ER
COPYRIGHT © 1996 THE ESTATE OF W.A.POUCHER
ISBN 0 09 475570 1
PRINTED IN HONG KONG THROUGH WORLD PRINT LTD.

A CIP CATALOGUE RECORD FOR THIS BOOK IS AVAILABLE FROM
THE BRITISH LIBRARY

CONTENTS

PREFACE

My late father was a regular visitor to Scotland for a period of over forty years and during this time he amassed a large collection of both black and white negatives and colour transparencies covering the area. In the 1940s he produced five books of monochrome photographs of the Scottish mountain scene, four of which have long been out of print; in 1980 a second edition of the fifth, *The Magic of Skye* was published by Constable and the book, now in its third edition, is still available. His guidebook *The Scottish Peaks* appeared in 1964 and is now in its seventh edition.

Finally, during the 1980s four books of colour photographs were published: *Scotland*, *The Highlands of Scotland*, *Skye* and *The Magic of the Highlands*. As all of these are now either out of print or will shortly be so, the publishers suggested that, from the large collection of colour transparencies of Scotland passed to me by my father, I select some of the best, not excluding those that had already appeared in print, to form the present volume, the publication of which will enable a new generation of lovers of Scotland's picturesque scenery to have a permanent record of some of the magnificent views that the mountainous areas of this beautiful country have to offer.

In consultation with Constable I have selected one hundred photographs which we consider to be 'The Best of Poucher's Scotland'. I have arranged these photographs using the same plan adopted by my father, that is beginning on the Isle of Arran moving over to the mainland at Loch Lomond, then weaving a way up the western side of the country, around the northern extremity and back down the eastern side, finally ending with a tour round the Isle of Skye from Kyleakin, north through Trotternish and south to Dunvegan, the Coolins, Elgol and Tarskavaig.

The map which appears on pages 10 and 11 has been included so that readers can follow the sequence of photographs in the book and also note their location on the ground so they can, if they so wish, go and take their own photographs.

John Poucher
Gate Ghyll,
High Brigham,
Cockermouth,
Cumbria
1996

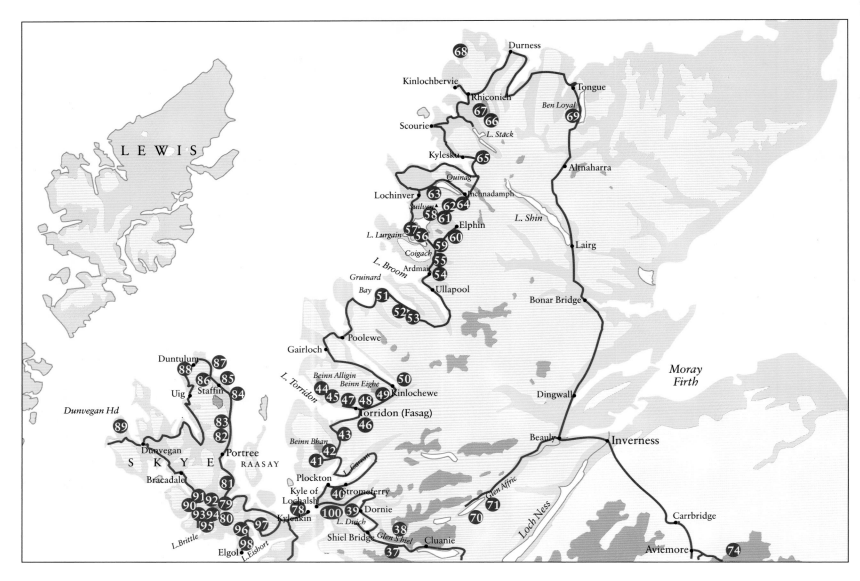

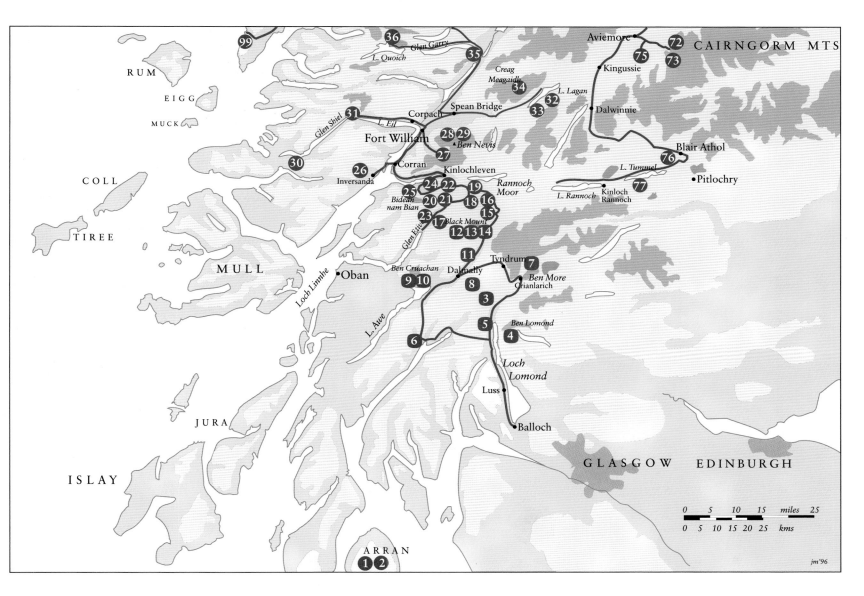

THE ARRAN HILLS
FROM BRODICK

[1]

These hills occupy the northern half of this
beautiful island and the three ridges are
dominated by Goat Fell. This peak can easily
be ascended by anyone who is fit, and the walk
to the north along its summit ridge opens up
the finest views of the central ridge backed by the
distant sea.

THE ARRAN HILLS FROM BRODICK

THE PINNACLED RIDGE OF GOAT FELL

[2]

Walking along this lofty ridge on a clear sunny
morning reveals a splendid prospect of the most
picturesque peaks of Arran.

BEN VORLICH
FROM LOCH LOMOND

[3]

Dominated by Ben Lomond this loch lies almost on the doorstep of Glasgow and is a prize for lovers of beautiful scenery. It is the largest sheet of fresh water in Britain, and covers an area of nearly twenty-seven and a half square miles. While the island-studded lower reaches of the loch are largely given up to water-sports of all kinds, its upper reaches are narrow and altogether more charming to the eye. The road along its western banks yields the finest scenery, of which this photograph is typical.

BEN LOMOND
FROM LOCH LOMOND

[4]
Less than an hour's drive from Glasgow,
Ben Lomond broods peacefully over its
shining loch, the most famous in Scotland.
A well-trodden track provides easy ascent of this
southernmost 'Munro' (or 3,000-ft peak), from
Rowardennan on Loch Lomond's eastern shore.

THE COBBLER

[5]

This is the name given by the climbing fraternity to Ben Arthur which rises to the north-west of Loch Long. Its weird serrated profile at once stamps it as the most striking peak in the southern Highlands, and it is well seen from the railway in the vicinity of Arrochar. Its summit ridge can be reached by a good path from Succoth, but the central peak involves some rock climbing and should not be attempted by the lone walker.

LOCH FYNE
AND INVERARAY

[6]
Inveraray is the ancient home of the
Clan Campbell. The present village dates from
1746 and is a fine example of eighteenth-century
town planning. The unusual large white gateways
add to the tidy and attractive appearance of
the village.

BEN MORE
FROM STRATH FILLAN

[7]

This beautifully shaped mountain is a
conspicuous landmark throughout the length of
Glen Dochart and Strath Fillan, and, together
with its equally graceful neighbour Stobinian,
affords one of the easiest ascents in Perthshire,
provided always that the atmosphere is clear and
the peak is not snowbound. It is the highest peak
in Britain south of Strathtay, and in consequence
discloses a stupendous panorama on a clear day.

BEN LUI AND
BEINN A'CHLEIBH

[8]

These two mountains dominate the southern slopes of Glen Lochy, and their traverse from Tyndrum to Dalmally makes an exhilarating walk.

Ben Lui and
Beinn a'Chleibh

BEN CRUACHAN
FROM LOCH AWE

[9]

Ben Cruachan is the highest of the eight tops
crowning this great mountain range, which is
bounded on the north by the deep rift of
Glen Noe and on the south by Loch Awe and
the Pass of Brander. It covers an area of about
twenty square miles and forms a horseshoe
stretching some four miles from east to west.
The long walk along these lofty ridges is one
of the finest in this part of Scotland.

GLEN ORCHY FALLS

[11]

A narrow road leaves Glen Lochy near Dalmally
to make a shorter connection with the highway
across Rannoch Moor, and it follows the burn all
the way. There is a large lay-by opposite the falls,
which are the finest hereabouts.

THE BLACKMOUNT
FROM RANNOCH MOOR

[12]

Any traveller driving from Tyndrum to
Fort William cannot fail to be impressed by the
vast desolation of Rannoch Moor, as the A82 road
passes through some of the grandest scenery in the
Scottish Highlands for no less than thirty miles.
Of these, about twelve miles consist of wild,
undulating moorland, triangular in shape and
stretching from Loch Tulla to Altnafeadh, with
its apex on Loch Rannoch. Those who have tried
to walk across it in any direction will have some
conception of the Moor's immensity and of the
pitfalls that are unexpectedly encountered; for it
is intersected by many burns, cradles some
large lochs and innumerable small lochans, and
abounds in peat hags and areas of impossible
bog. To attempt to cross it in clear weather is a
hazardous adventure, but in rain and mist it
could spell disaster. In fact, to be parachuted into
the centre of Rannoch Moor in such conditions
would present a problem of escape to test the
stamina and skill of our toughest commandos.
Yet on a sunny day, Rannoch Moor is resplendent
with wild beauty, engirdled by mountains and
decked with glittering sheets of water, which,
together with boulders strewn about and great
masses of heather, make a picture that apppeals
to both artist and photographer.

THE BLACKMOUNT
FROM RANNOCH MOOR

[13]

Whereas the last photograph was taken on a
wild and stormy autumn day, this one, shot from
a very similar viewpoint, shows almost the
same view in calmer, early winter conditions.
The major peak on the left of the picture is
Stob Ghabhar (peak of the goats) and in the
centre is Coire Ba, one of the largest and grandest
corries in the Highlands.

STOB GHABHAR
FROM LOCH TULLA

[14]

The southern peak of the Blackmount frowns upon the head of this lovely loch, which is seen at its best from the by-road to Victoria Bridge. Stob Ghabhar is the first hill to be climbed when making the magnificent traverse of this fine mountain group.

CLACH LEATHAD AND MEALL A'BHUIRAIDH FROM THE MOOR

[15]

This picture shows the most spectacular view of the Moor from a roadside lochan.

SRON NA CREISE
FROM KINGSHOUSE

[16]

Here is a splendid view of the terminal peaks of
the Blackmount as seen from Kingshouse.
This hostelry, on the old Glencoe road, is an
excellent centre for the exploration of the
Glencoe district.

A Charming Lochan
in Glen Etive

[17]

Perhaps the most picturesque feature of this
long and lovely glen is the small lochan portrayed
here. It lies some distance to the left of the road
and may be reached by a sketchy path which
terminates in a fine mass of rhododendrons, seen
at their best in May.

A Charming Lochan
in Glen Etive

BUACHAILLE ETIVE MOR
EMERGING FROM
THE MORNING MIST

[18]

This shapely peak is known as the 'Shepherd of
Etive' and is seen at its best from near
Kingshouse. It is famous for its many difficult
rock climbs and is a favourite with all
mountaineers.

GLENCOE FROM THE OLD ROAD

[19]

This photograph displays the Three Sisters of
Glencoe to perfection, but it does not reveal the
summit of Bidean nam Bian which is hidden
behind the slopes of Beinn Fhada on the left.
The conspicuous top on the right, which is often
mistaken for it, is in fact Stob Coire nan Lochan.

AONACH DUBH
FROM CLACHAIG

[20]

Crowned by Stob Coire nan Lochan, this is the third of the famous Sisters and is seen at its best from Clachaig. The break in the centre of the cliffs is known as the 'Dinner-time Buttress', and it affords a quick ascent for the experienced climber.

STOB COIRE
NAN LOCHAN

[21]

Looking towards the south side of Glencoe from
the Aonach Eagach ridge, you see this superb
view of Stob Coire nan Lochan whose summit is
lifted high by its two outliers, Gearr Aonach and
Aonach Dubh.

AONACH EAGACH –
THE NORTH WALL
OF GLENCOE

[22]

This spectacular ridge is one of the narrowest and most exciting in the central Highlands. But its traverse is the special preserve of the experienced climber, and once on it, there is no escape from the crest except at either end.

BIDEAN NAM BIAN
FROM LOCH LEVEN

[23]
Instead of crossing the bridge at Ballachulish,
it is worthwhile driving round this beautiful
sea-loch. It opens up a succession of lovely views
of the enclosing hills, one of the best of which is
seen in this picture.

[24]

As mentioned in the caption to the last photograph, many beautiful scenes are unveiled from the road along the north side of Loch Leven including this view of the Pap of Glencoe which is the western sentinel of Aonach Eagach.

LOCH LEVEN AND THE PAP OF GLENCOE

LOCH LEVEN AND
THE HILLS OF ARDGOUR

[25]

The still waters of Loch Leven perfectly
mirror the faraway hills of Ardgour. It is not
often that the Highland scene is as sweetly
sunlit as this – the area has one of the highest
rainfall figures for the whole of Britain!

GARBH BHEINN ON A WILD DAY

[26]

A seven mile walk over the group starts at the
bridge across the burn flowing down Glen Iubhair.
The route circles the glen, and by walking to
the right of it, uphill to Druim an Iubhair and
its lochan, a splendid prospect of the peak is
revealed. This shot was taken on a wild day, but
the side-lighting clearly shows the Great Gully.

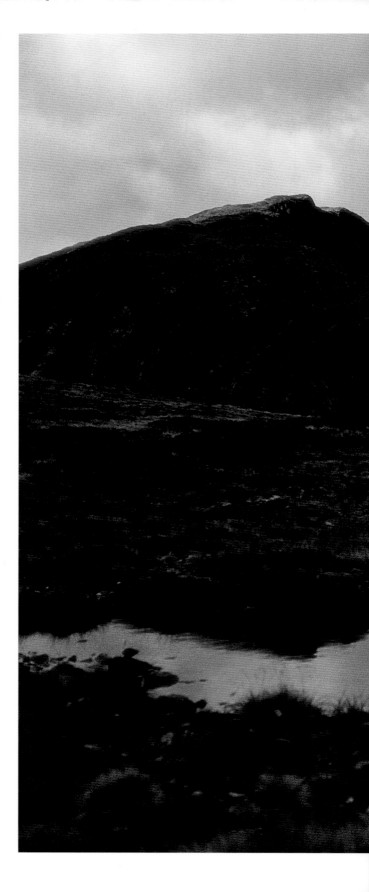

THE MAMORE PEAKS
FROM GLEN NEVIS

[27]

The reward of a drive from Fort William to this glen is the superb scenery for which it is famous. On approaching Polldubh the first glimpse of Mamore Forest is disclosed, with Sgurr a'Mhaim and Stob Ban topping the skyline, as seen in this picture.

BEN NEVIS
FROM BANAVIE

[28]

Sunshine highlights the rugged profile of the
monarch of Britain's peaks, which is estimated
to have only about twenty clear days a year!
If you are lucky enough to reach the summit on
one of those days, your view across the encircling
hills will be unsurpassed, for you will be standing
more than 4,400 feet above sea level.

BEN NEVIS
FROM CORPACH

[29]

Corpach village lies at the southern end of the old Caledonian Canal, and its buildings on the pier make a charming foreground to this view of the great Ben on the other side of Loch Linnhe.

[30]

The prominence of this mountain, which is seen here from the narrow terminus of Loch Shiel, is owing to its relative isolation on low ground between Lochs Shiel and Sunart. Though it can be climbed from many directions, the approach to it from Resipol Farm on Loch Sunart is the most popular.

THE GLENFINNAN MONUMENT

[31]
There can be few more familiar scenes in the
Highlands of Scotland than this one – the
monument to Prince Charles Edward Stuart at
the head of Loch Shiel. The monument is owned
by the National Trust for Scotland, and their
Visitors Centre nearby tells the story of the
Prince and the 1745 Rising which he led.

LOCH LAGGAN

[32]
This loch is some twelve miles in length, and its waters are used as a reservoir by the British Aluminium Company at their works outside Fort William.

LOCH LAGGAN AND
BINNEIN SHUAS

[33]

The dark mass of Binnein Shuas broods behind
the still waters of Loch Laggan against a
thundery sky, the sombreness of the scene being
relieved by the brilliant autumn colours in the
foreground. Though large parts of the Highlands
nowadays are covered with commercial pine
forests, broad leaved gems like the trees in this
picture still add glorious hues to the landscape,
and delight the photographer.

CREAG MEAGAIDH

[34]
The large mass of this mountain to the west of
Loch Laggan looks rather unexceptional from the
lochside road. But the motorist prepared to leave
the car and don a pair of walking boots can see
its hidden gem – the spectacular Coire Ardair,
attained after a fair walk along an often
boggy track.

GOLDEN DAYS
IN GLEN GARRY

[35]

Before the level of this loch was raised, it was famous for the birches which decked its northern shore for miles. Unhappily thousands of them perished in the process, and one can only hope they will grow again in the coming years, to reproduce this lovely golden tapestry.

LOCH QUOICH

[36]
The road to Kinloch Hourn keeps to the loch's northern shore for miles; this photograph was taken about halfway along the immense stretch of water, fully revealing the splendour of its situation.

FAOCHAG AND THE SADDLE FROM GLEN SHIEL

[37]

The drive down this famous glen is a delight, with the hills closing in until the two peaks shown here appear to block its exit. However, on crossing the Bridge of Shiel the road bears left to skirt the flanks of the Saddle, until the waters of Loch Duich appear ahead. This picture is the classic view of the wild scene.

THE FIVE SISTERS
OF KINTAIL

[38]

This magnificent range dominates the head of Loch Duich, and this photograph, taken from the crest of Mam Rattachan, shows their finest elevation, as well as including the blue of the loch. Today, the trees in the foreground have grown so high that the peaks on the right of the picture only just overtop them. The complete traverse of this long range is a considerable undertaking, even with transport to a point in Glen Shiel immediately below the Belach an Lapain, where the east-to-west route begins. If completed, it involves 10,000 feet of ascent and descent.

EILEAN DONAN CASTLE

[39]

One of Scotland's most easily recognisable
fortresses, Eilean Donan is sited near Dornie,
alongside the road to the Kyle of Lochalsh,
gateway to Skye. It was blown up in 1719 by an
English warship after the battle of Glen Shiel but
subsequently restored. As seen here, the castle's
situation at the point where Lochs Duich and
Long merge and flow into Loch Alsh, is truly
majestic, and a fitting memorial to Clan MacRae.

PLOCKTON

[40]

This charming fishing and crofting village,
part of the Balmacara estate, is most beautifully
situated on a small inlet of Loch Carron and
provides excellent views of the wild
Applecross mountains to the north. It is worthy
of a visit, and can most easily be reached from
the Kyle of Lochalsh.

PLOCKTON

THE SATELLITES OF BEINN BHAN

[41]

During the descent to Loch Kishorn by the hill-road from Loch Carron, this fine mountain scene comes into view. On the right of Sgurr a'Chaorachain stands the Cioch, a famous problem for the rock climber. The spectacular road to Applecross starts at Tornapress, and at first rises gently across the area of open moorland, seen in the foreground of this picture, before entering the defile of the Allt a' Chumhaing, where it becomes steeper, with the cliffs of Meall Gorm on the left, and of Sgurr a' Chaorachain on the right; in a distance of only six miles it rises from sea-level to a height of 2,053 feet at the Bealach na Ba, its final zig-zags climbing at a gradient of 1 in 3. But the road is safe, and is a *must* for touring motorists. Until 1970, when the well-engineered road round the north of the peninsula was opened, this was the only vehicular access to the village of Applecross and it can be imagined how isolated its population must have felt in severe winter conditions when deep snow made it impassable.

BEINN BHAN

[42]
The satellites of this mountain rise spectacularly
above Loch Kishorn, but the four castellated
corries facing the north-east, and seen only
distantly from the narrow road to Shieldaig, are
its finest feature, and well worth a close inspection.
To reach them easily, follow the stalker's path
which starts beyond the river-bridge at
Tornapress and skirts the south-east shoulder
of the mountain. When the corries appear
high up on the left, walk up to them over the
heathery slopes that lead to Coire na Feola,
which is seen in this picture.

94

BEINN DAMH FROM LOCH AN LOIN

[43]

The narrow road to Shieldaig passes this small loch, which is one of the viewpoints that best reveals the long summit ridge of Beinn Damh. A remarkable feature is the strange 'Stirrup Mark' below the summit, whose prominence is due to white quartzite scree.

BEINN ALLIGIN FROM THE RIVER BALGY

[44]

Rising in Loch Damh, this famous river flows down to Loch Torridon through five salmon pools and here, when used as a foreground, provides a delightful contrast to the brooding mass of Beinn Alligin, behind.

COIRE MHIC NOBUIL AND BEINN ALLIGIN

[45]
The wild reaches of this glen, with its babbling
burn tumbling down to meet Loch Torridon, are
a perfect vantage-point for the great northern
corries of Liathach and the delightful profile of
Beinn Alligin, 'jewel of Torridon'. The 'Horns'
of Alligin are visible on the skyline directly
behind the bridge.

THE COULIN AND BEINN DAMH FORESTS FROM THE DIABAIG ROAD

[46]

One of the most beautiful drives in the Torridon area is to the remote village of Diabaig – the single-track road runs for miles high above Loch Torridon, and from it can be seen many peaks of the Coulin and Beinn Damh Forests, of which Beinn Damh is the most prominent.

LIATHACH
FROM INVER ALLIGIN

[47]

From this little hamlet nestling on the shore of
Loch Torridon, immediately below Beinn Alligin,
there is an outstanding view of the 'end-on'
prospect of Liathach.

LIATHACH
FROM LOCH CLAIR

[48]
This is the classic view from Loch Clair of the
truly magnificent sandstone giant, Liathach.
The climber does well to treat with respect its
airy ridge under snow – the main problem is the
serrated pinnacles of Am Fasarinen which must
be negotiated with extreme care if the climber
wishes to avoid hurtling hundreds of feet into
the wild corries below.

BEINN EIGHE
FROM LOCH COULIN

[49]

Some half-way along Glen Torridon there are
two lovely lochs. Loch Clair lies beside the road
at the foot of Beinn Eighe (which is the largest of
the Torridon peaks, and a complete range in
itself) and to the south of it lies Loch Coulin,
which may be reached by a level private road.
Loch Coulin is the best place from which to
appraise Beinn Eighe, as is shown in this picture.
The great mountain is scenically outstanding
for two reasons: first, tremendous areas of
white quartzite scree are draped over its
higher slopes and glitter like snow on a
sunny day; and second, Coire Mhic Fhearchair
lies on the north-western extremity of the range
and is undoubtedly the most magnificent
in all Scotland.

A clearly marked path rises gently from the
car-park in the glen, passes through the
narrow gap between the two adjoining peaks,
and steepens as it approaches the corrie. It is
hard going for the elderly and takes about
two hours, but the rewards are immense, for its
three buttresses, of which the lower halves consist
of red sandstone and the upper halves of
white quartzite, rise into the sky on the far side
of the corrie to frown upon the lonely lochan
at their feet.

SLIOCH
FROM GRUDIE BRIDGE

[50]

This well-known bridge is six miles from
Kinlochewe and is a good viewpoint for Slioch,
whose bold, square, castellated summit looks
most attractive under snow. But in summery
conditions it is clearly seen in splendid isolation,
dominating miles of the upper reaches of
Loch Maree.

GRUINARD BAY

[51]

After leaving behind the attractive gardens at Inverewe, the road enters a long section of wild country, often flanked by the sea. Its jewel is the lovely bay which suddenly appears far below, at a bend where cars may be parked. Beyond it, on the distant horizon to the right, is the first glimpse of An Teallach, another of Scotland's great mountains.

An Teallach from the Road of Destitution

[52]

This great mountain range, with its lofty
pinnacled ridge, is seen at its best from the road
a few miles to the east of Dundonnell. Its traverse
is one of the mountaineer's treasured experiences,
but should not be attempted by ordinary walkers.

TOLL AN LOCHAIN

[53]

An Teallach is one of the most spectacular mountains in the Highlands and vies in splendour with Liathach in Torridon. Its main ridge, some three miles long, throws out three spurs to the east: these enclose two magnificent corries, of which Toll an Lochain is pictured here. The photograph, taken in early morning light, clearly shows the steepness of its cliffs, the serrated skyline ridge, and the lochan nearly 2,000 feet below. The traverse of the ridge goes from right to left, and the skyline peaks in that order are: Sgurr Fiona, Lord Berkeley's Seat, Corrag Bhuidhe Pinnacles, and Corrag Bhuidhe Buttress.

BEN MORE COIGACH
FROM ARDMAIR BAY

[54]

One of the most beautiful bays in this part of the
Highlands, where a few isolated cottages stand
on the curving shore that leads the eye to the
long ridge of Ben More Coigach. This can easily
be traversed by any fit walker.

BEN MORE COIGACH FROM A DRUMRUNIE LOCHAN

[55]

This sequestered little sheet of water lies beside
the road and can easily be missed by a motorist
driving fast. When its gleaming surface is still,
it mirrors all the surrounding peaks: one of them
is seen in this picture.

THE APPROACH TO
STAC POLLY

[56]

Fourteen miles from Ullapool, this little
Coigach peak stands alone above the waters of
Loch Lurgain, and is reached by a single-track
road that turns left at Drumrunie from the main
highway to Ledmore. There are distant views
of the mountain long before the turn, but only on
approaching the loch is its elevation seen to full
advantage, as in this, my favourite, picture of it.

STAC POLLY

[57]

This little peak can now easily be ascended by the zig-zag path on its northern slopes, enabling visitors of any age to reach its summit ridge. The bristling sandstone pinnacles make it an irresistable subject for the photographer, who in favourable weather can capture them backed by many blue lochans far below. There is a car-park at the starting point of the ascent. This picture was taken on an autumn afternoon.

SUILVEN FROM THE WESTERN TOWERS

[58]

From this vantage-point on Stac Polly,
the climber can look north and see Suilven
between its two imposing western towers.

CUL BEAG
FROM LOCH LURGAIN

[59]
The placing of the boat on the sandy shore of the little cove makes the picture.

[60]

Suilven is wedge-shaped, and rises in splendid isolation from the lochan-strewn moors of Sutherland. Seen here from the east, near Cam Loch, it presents a sharp, tapering and inaccessible appearance, whereas from the west near Lochinver its lofty summit is rounded. Its summit ridge is one and a half miles long, and climbers must walk about five miles to reach the gully that gives easy access to the Bealach Mor, where the traverse begins.

THE LONG RIDGE OF SUILVEN FROM THE SOUTH

[61]
Taken on the path from Inverkirkaig, this picture shows clearly the surprising length, and the sharp undulations, of Suilven's summit ridge.

CANISP AND SUILVEN FROM THE DRUMBEG SCENIC DRIVE

[62]

A picturesque drive starts at Lochinver and circles the coast to the north, passing the remote hamlet of Drumbeg, crossing the moors to Skaig Bridge, and returning along the shore of Loch Assynt. It unveils many lovely views of the sea, and a visit to the lighthouse at Stoer is a worthwhile diversion. This photograph was taken in retrospect from the first hill on the circuit.

THE RIVER INVER

[63]

Famous for its salmon, this river takes root at the outflow of Loch Assynt and reaches the sea at Lochinver. In my early days it was common to see no cars other than Rolls-Royces and Bentleys parked beside it at the favourite beats for salmon-fisherman. But not so today. On a sunny autumn afternoon, its waters flow through a golden tapestry of great beauty, and lead the eye to the Sail Ghorm ridge of Quinag.

QUINAG AND
ARDVRECK CASTLE
FROM LOCH ASSYNT

[64]

Lochs and lochans of great charm and in
beautiful settings are dotted about all over
Scotland, and many of them are an irresistable
magnet for salmon- and trout-fishermen.
It would be invidious for me to declare any one
of them the most beautiful, but I always take a
special delight in visiting Loch Assynt. It is
dominated by the great mountain of Quinag, and
is also famous for the ruin of Ardvreck Castle
which stands on its shore – Montrose was
confined here in a dungeon before being taken to
Edinburgh for execution. There is a good hotel
at Inchnadamph near its head and another at
Lochinver not far from the outflow of this lovely
Sutherland loch. Scenery on the grand scale can
be enjoyed by driving in any direction for a
few miles: perhaps the drive to Kylesku is best
of all.

QUINAG AND ARDVRECK CASTLE FROM LOCH ASSYNT

LOCH GLENDHUI
FROM KYLESKU

[65]

This large loch runs due east from Kylesku, and
is famous for its brilliant reflection of the sunrise.
But, as seen here, its still waters can also mirror
the silvery clouds.

ARKLE
FROM LOCH STACK

[66]

This loch is said to be rich in salmon, and it lies
between Ben Stack and Arkle. The latter mountain
consisting of quartzite, is known to mountaineers
as a 'Slag Heap' – not worthy of exploration.

ARKLE
FROM LOCH STACK

A DISTANT VIEW OF FOINAVEN

[67]

This group of hills, straddling vast
moorland solitudes in the north of Sutherland,
is too remote to become popular with
mountain walkers. During the drive from Scourie,
Foinaven, as seen here, suddenly appears on the
distant horizon, but it can only be reached by
crossing immense tracts of bog from a point
some miles to the north of Rhiconich.

SANDWOOD BAY

[68]

This bay, some distance to the south of
Cape Wrath, is regarded by many as the most
picturesque in Scotland. It can be reached from
Kinlochbervie by car, followed by an easy walk.

BEN LOYAL
FROM LOCHAN HACOIN

[69]

This superb mountain rises from the swelling moorland some five miles to the south of Tongue, and its western front, when seen from the vicinity of Lochan Hacoin, makes one of the most striking pictures in Britain. Known also as the 'Queen of Scottish peaks', it is admired alike by artists and photographers. Its particular splendour is due to the graceful pendant ridges that join its four western peaks of granite; they impart to the whole of it a grandeur that is altogether out of proportion to its height.

GLEN AFFRIC

[70]
The public road to this world-famous glen
begins in Strath Glas and follows Chisholm's Pass
above the Dog Falls to the eastern end of
Loch Benevian, seen here. Glen Affric should be
visited, if possible, in the autumn, when millions
of gold-leaved birches make a glorious picture.

LOCH BENEVIAN

[71]

The beauty of this glorious loch is owed in part
to the absence of the lateral moraine that mars
so many of Britains lakes. This is because the
waters of Loch Mullardoch in the adjoining
Glen Cannich flow through a tunnel into
Glen Affric and automatically 'top up'
Loch Benevian – a clever idea developed by the
Scottish Hydro-electric Board. Raising the level
of the loch has meant abandoning the old road
along its shore.

THE NORTHERN CORRIES OF CAIRNGORM FROM LOCH MORLICH

[72]

The shores of Loch Morlich, on the road between Aviemore and the Cairngorm ski-slopes, command an unsurpassed view of the northern corries of Cairngorm. From left to right they are Coire Cas, Coire an t'Sneachda and Coire an Lochain. The area has been the centre of a storm of controversy in recent years over the extent of development for skiing.

THE CLIFFS
OF CAIRN LOCHAN

[73]

The cliffs of this great corrie, part of the Cairn
Gorm range, are perhaps the most magnificent in
the region (this long ridge and its corries can be
seen in the previous photograph). Mountain
walkers can reach the cairn on Cairn Gorm by
the chairlift in Coire Cas, and from there can
enjoy a splendid walk along the crest of Stob
Coire an t'Sneachda to the cairn on the very edge
of Cairn Lochan, where precipitous cliffs enclose
Coire an Lochain with two tiny lochans at their
base. As the cliffs face north-west, the
spectacular scene can only be photographed
satisfactorily when they are lit by the declining
sun.

AN LOCHAN UAINE,
RYVOAN

[74]

A short walk from Glenmore Lodge, near which
a car may be parked, brings one to this
enchanting lochan. Sitting beside it on a calm day
is a rewarding pleasure for the explorer of these
massive hills.

THE CASTLE
OF LOCH AN EILEAN

[75]

This small loch is only a short distance from
Aviemore, and is one of the chief attractions of
the district.

THE QUEEN'S VIEW, LOCH TUMMEL

[76]

The magnificent peak of Schiehallion (3,547 feet) dominates the scenery of central Perthshire, the ancient lands of Breadalbane. A parking place on the B8019 road a few miles out of Pitlochry commands the 'Queen's View' seen here, which is named after a visit made by Queen Victoria in 1866. The eye is drawn down the lovely length of Loch Tummel to the peak rearing up against the distant skyline.

SCHIEHALLION

[77]

Loch Rannoch is ten miles long and the centre of an outstandingly beautiful area. Looking eastwards, Schiehallion appears as a perfect cone, framed by the trees. Its shape led to the mountain's being used by Maskelyne, an eighteenth-century Astronomer Royal, in experiments to determine the mass of the earth.

I think it is true to say that Skye is our most beautiful island and, with the exception of Sleat, it consists of barren undulating moorland from which rise our most spectacular mountains, the Coolins. Sleat is its most southerly peninsula and is usually regarded as the 'Garden of Skye', with more natural forest than the rest of the landscape. The whole coastline is indented by many lovely blue sea-lochs, and in fact no place is more than four or five miles from the sea. Its metropolis is the small, busy town of Portree, from which good roads radiate to every corner of the island and whose main connection with the mainland is the bridge, opened on 16 October 1995, which from Kyle of Lochalsh, with its road and rail links with Inverness, passes over Kyle Akin and terminates near Kyleakin.

This misty isle is the Mecca of all British mountaineers, for there are no other great mountains (save perhaps Liathach and An Teallach) to compete with its serrated main ridge twisting southwards from Sligachan to Glen Brittle on the Atlantic coast. Innumerable pinnacles project from its narrow crest, whose traverse is too difficult for any save the experienced mountaineer.

This should not deter the walker or the motorist from visiting Skye, for they will delight in the picturesque landscape and in the engirdling sea-cliffs which are, in places, nearly 1,000 feet high. After crossing the bridge from Kyle of Lochalsh, the traveller should follow the coast road for about twenty-five miles, first passing through Broadford and then, with the Red Hills on the left, finally swinging round to Sligachan, which is dominated by the splendour of Sgurr nan Gillean. Here he will find a first-class hotel which in my early days was patronised only by mountaineers and fishermen, whereas today it is the favoured hostelry of touring motorists. From its very doors the visitor can walk along Glen Sligachan to Loch Coruisk, with splendid hills on either side and a spectacular terminus of unparalleled wild beauty; or he can cross the low pass to Glen Brittle with the towering peaks of the Black Coolins on his left all the way.

Should he prefer a drive, there is the complete circuit of the northern peninsula of Trotternish – the finest in Skye. The road goes north from Portree, passes below the precipices of the Storr with its conspicuous Old Man of Storr, runs for miles along the edge of the sea-cliffs, passes near Quiraing with its weird pinnacles, and then Flodigarry, one-time home of Flora MacDonald. Thence it follows the coast to the western side of Trotternish, with glimpses of the ruined castle of Duntulm, followed by Kilmuir with Flora MacDonald's monument and then Uig with its graceful bay. Beyond this a splendid road leads him back to Portree.

KYLEAKIN

[78]

Kyleakin is a small port which is dominated by the ruins of Castle Moil. Before it was bypassed by the construction of the bridge over Kyle Akin, it was the terminus of the ferry service from Kyle of Lochalsh. However, for visitors not using the bridge, there are two ferries still in operation, the larger one from Mallaig to Armadale, and the smaller, in the summer only, between Glenelg and Kylerhea.

GLAMAIG

[79]
The burn makes a wonderful foreground for a
picture of the symmetrical cone of this mountain,
which lies within easy reach of Sligachan.
Any walker who is full of energy can try reaching
its mossy summit within an hour – and will be
rewarded by a splendid panorama.

MARSCO FROM THE SLIGACHAN BURN

[80]

This shapely peak rises in isolation from the wilderness of Glen Sligachan and is one of its best-known landmarks. It is further down the glen than it looks from the hotel, but it may be ascended by any walker if he is accompanied by a climber who knows the terrain.

RAINBOW OVER THE PORTREE ROAD

[81]

This magical scene appeared before me as I was
driving to Portree one day after a storm. Skye lies
in the path of the warm south-westerly winds
which condense as they are blown against its
cold hillsides, and which produce the
great cloudscapes so characteristic of the
Misty Isle.

THE STORR FROM
THE STAFFIN ROAD

[82]

Leaving Portree, the road runs north as we begin
our round of Trotternish. This brooding winter
scene of icy roads and snowy peaks was taken
just before Christmas.

THE STORR FROM LOCH FADA

[83]

By contrast with the preceding picture, a bright summer day gave me this perfect 'classic' shot of the Bastions of the Storr frowning down on the little loch.

THE KILT ROCK

[84]

Continuing along the Staffin road, you will come upon Loch Mealt lying almost on the verge of the great sea-cliffs. Only a few yards' walk brings you to the sensational overhang and reveals the superbly rifted Kilt Rock whose columns resemble the basaltic pillars of Staffa. Care is essential when taking photographs of it from the very edge of the cliffs, with the sea hundreds of feet below.

STAFFIN BAY

[85]

Further north still, you will find this charming, almost semi-circular bay where you may linger in tranquility and turn your eyes to the far horizon to gaze at the distant mainland mountains.

QUIRAING

[86]

To the west of Staffin Bay lies another fantastic group of towers and buttresses. Most climbers visiting Skye tend to concentrate on the Coolin ridge, but the journey north through Portree to Quiraing can be equally rewarding, especially for devotees of the unusual.

STRANGE SHAPES

[87]

The height, the solitude, the weird dark pinnacles, the extensive views – this picture, perhaps, summarises the secret and lonely joys of Quiraing.

DUNTULM CASTLE
FROM THE WEST

[88]

This historic ruin occupies an impregnable
position overlooking the sea, but from its
southern side it can easily be reached and
explored. The castle was formerly a stronghold of
the Macdonalds of the Isles, and was the
successor to Dunscaith Castle, near Isle Ornsay.

DUNVEGAN HEAD

[89]

Frowning over the waters of Loch Pooltiel are the
beetling cliffs of Dunvegan Head. They contain
one most unusual feature – a waterfall that
apparently plummets straight into the sea.

Dunvegan Head

SGURR NAN GILLEAN FROM SLIGACHAN

[90]

As those who have passed through Sligachan will know, it is dominated by Sgurr nan Gillean and its adjacent peaks. The viewpoint for this photograph, showing the outline of the mountains faithfully mirrored in a small lochan, will be found not far from the hotel.

S NOW ON THE NORTHERN COOLINS

[91]

This scene, familiar to climbers who love Skye, was taken from the small lochan on the left of the Carbost road just above Sligachan; it shows Sgurr nan Gillean prominent on the left, with the peaks on its right huddled together as far as Bruach na Frithe.

GILLEAN SEEN
THROUGH CLOUDS

[92]
This is an unusual portrait of Gillean and its
satellites, for in years of visits to Skye I have only
seen such a wreath of clouds on one occasion.

GILLEAN SEEN
THROUGH CLOUDS

COIRE NA CREICHE

[93]

One of the most magnificent corries in the Coolins, this is seen at its best from the path to Glen Brittle. Its central peak, Sgurr an Fheadain, is split vertically by the famous Waterpipe Gully, and is crowned by Bidein Druim nan Ramh, one of the tricky obstacles encountered during the traverse of the Main Ridge.

[94]

The evening sunlight beautifully illuminates the
lower slopes of Sgurr nan Gobhar, seen here to
advantage in an 'end-on' view from the moorland
north of Glen Brittle.

COIRE LAGAN

[95]

Sgurr Alasdair is the highest peak in the Coolins, and its ascent is usually made by way of the famous Stone Shoot which falls into this corrie. A walker can attain the corrie by a path from Glen Brittle, but few attempt the tough ascent of the Stone Shoot. Coire Lagan is a wonderful place in which to linger after a day on the ridges, and is so fascinating that many climbers have had to descend to the glen in the dark.

BLAVEN
FROM LOCH SLAPIN

[96]

The long hilly drive from Broadford to Elgol
unveils some magnificent views, and is a *must* for
all visitors to Skye. This first dramatic scene
appears on the approach to Loch Slapin,
where the grandeur of the mountain group
beyond it is seen at its best. The lofty ridges of
Blaven, Clach Glas, and Sgurr nan Each make
one of the finest rock traverses on the island.

BEINN NA CRO
REFLECTED IN
LOCH SLAPIN

[97]
A charming scene is revealed in retrospect
from the cottage standing on the edge of the loch,
near its narrows.

THE COOLINS
FROM ELGOL

[98]

This superb spectacle of the Coolins is suddenly
disclosed at the end of the road to Elgol,
looking across the immense blue foreground of
Loch Scavaig. When seen in favourable conditions,
as in this picture, it is considered by connoisseurs
as one of the finest in the world.

THE COOLINS
FROM TARSKAVAIG

[99]

Tarskavaig in the west of Sleat, with
the frolicking waters of Loch Eishort in the
foreground, provides this splendid view of the
Black Coolins and their magnificent ridge – from
Gars-bheinn in the south to Sgurr nan Gillean
in the north. The soft, opalescent atmosphere
round the peaks is part of the characteristic
charm of Skye.

FAREWELL

[100]
The circular tour of this fascinating and
magical island ends where it began, at the
Kyle of Lochalsh, with a last look across the
blue waters to the misty mountains of Skye.
(It will be noted that this photograph was taken
before the bridge over the waters of Kyle Akin became
an alien intruder on this tranquil scene!)